Five Senses
Phonics

BOOK
6

Hunter Calder

A
FIVE SENSES
PUBLICATION

Five Senses Education Pty Ltd
2/195 Prospect Highway
Seven Hills NSW 2147 Australia
Phone   02 838 9265
Email   sevenhills@fivesenseseducation.com.au
Web   www.fivesenseseducation.com.au

Calder, Hunter
Five Senses Phonics Book 6
978-1-76032-427-8

2022 05 27

Contents

About the Author

Multiple award-winning author Hunter Calder has extensive experience as a reading teacher, consultant, teacher trainer and lecturer, both in Australia and overseas. He obtained a Master of Arts from the University of Sydney and a Master of Education from the University of New South Wales. His many publications include the acclaimed *Reading Freedom 2000* series and the *Excel Basic English* books. He also contributed to the *Literacy Planet* online program.

The *Five Senses Phonics* series of early literacy skills is his most recent series of phonics books and is the outcome of collaboration with the experienced people at Five Senses Education.

Introduction

Welcome to *Five Senses Phonics*, a carefully structured series of activity books for pre-readers and beginning readers at the important stage of their literacy acquisition. The Five Senses activity books are intended for use in a preschool setting, in the beginning school years, and for older students who are having difficulty learning to read.

Book 6 continues the development of essential reading skills — advanced phonics knowledge. Phonics applies a student's ability to hear and work with sounds in spoken words to reading them on the page. At this stage students learn to read words containing digraphs ('ar', 'er' 'or' and so on), diphthongs ('ow', 'oo' 'oi' and so on), and irregular word patterns ('air, 'igh', 'ow' and so on).

Once students have mastered the skills taught in Books 1–6 of the Five Senses Phonics program they are ready to learn the independent reading skills of syllabification (dividing words into syllables) and structural analysis (dividing words into prefixes-base words-suffixes). Once these skills are mastered student will have become independent readers.

Contemporary research tells us that students with good phonics skills go on to become competent readers. On the other hand, preschool age children and students in the early years at school who do not understand the relationship between spoken and written words are likely to develop literacy problems. Students who experience difficulty learning the skills of phonics may need the services of a specialised teacher trained in the development of auditory perception techniques.

Student progress should regularly be monitored and evaluated after completing each level, using the Achievement Tests section which is specifically designed for teachers to assess effectiveness and so students can see the positive results of their learning experiences.

Instructions for Book 6

Book 6 introduces students to higher order phonics skills — consonant digraphs, long vowel rules and soft 'e' and 'g' sounds. Because of this, the format for the introductory page of each unit targets specific skill.

Pages 1-5 — **Vowel and consonant sounds** — teach these sounds carefully and until students can reproduce them automatically.

Pages 6-11 — **Basic Sight Vocabulary** — these lists contain the basic sight words students need to work successfully with the program. Teach the words list by list until they are mastered, and once they are mastered regularly revise them. The basic sight words are presented at the bottom of each page so students can learn or revise them as they progress through the book.

Page 12 — **Introductory page** — teach the digraphs and diphthongs ('ow' as in 'clown' and so on). All words taught in this unit (except the sight words) contain the letter-sound correspondences learned in the earlier books.

Pages 13-22 — Students complete the activity pages that teach them to work with and read words containing digraphs and diphthongs.

Page 23-24 — Students display competence reading words containing digraphs and diphthongs.

Page 25 — **Introductory page** — Introduce the vowels before 'r' sounds. All words taught in this unit (except the sight words) contain the letter-sound correspondences learned in the earlier books.

Pages 26-35 — Students complete the activity pages that teach them to work with and read words containing the double vowel rule.

Page 37-38 — Students display competence reading words containing vowels before 'r'. All words taught in this unit (except the sight words) contain the letter-sound correspondences learned in the earlier books.

Page 39 — **Introductory page** — Introduce these irregular word patterns 'al' as in 'bald' and so on. All words taught in this unit (except the sight words) contain the letter-sound correspondences learned in the earlier books.

Sound Charts

Vowels

Say the sounds for these letters.

a as in

e as in

i as in

o as in

U as in

Sound Charts

Say the sounds for these letters.

b   as   in

c   as   in

d   as   in

f   as   in

g   as   in

(2)

Sound Charts

Say the sounds for these letters.

h   as   in

j   as   in

k   as   in

l   as   in

m   as   in

3

Sound Charts Consonants

Say the sounds for these letters.

n   as   in

p   as   in

r   as   in

s   as   in

t   as   in

4

Sound Charts Consonants

Say the sounds for these letters.

V as in

W as in

X as in

Y as in

Z as in

(5)

Sight Vocabulary

Learn these lists of sight words

a	in	and	saw	into	this
am	is	are	she	play	what
as	it	for	the	said	when
by	Mr	her	too	then	will
he	no	him	was	they	with
if	of	Mrs	why		
	on	not	yes		
		out	you		

Basic Sight Vocabulary

Can I read these words?

List One		List Two	
and	look	at	man
are	my	away	me
boy	of	big	not
can	play	blue	on
come	red	down	one
funny	run	for	ran
go	said	good	saw
he	says	green	three
is	see	have	too
jump	the	here	up
like	this	in	watch
little	to	it	you

 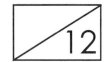 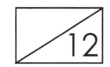 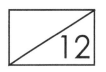

Yes I can!

Sight Words

Basic Sight Vocabulary

Can I read these words?

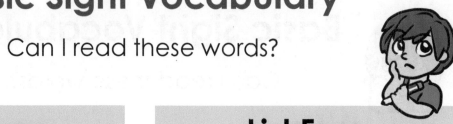

List Three		List Four	
all	going	an	had
am	home	after	help
around	into	as	her
black	make	be	him
but	no	brown	his
by	old	cold	if
call	out	did	she
came	was	ever	some
do	we	fly	stop
eat	will	from	two
fast	yellow	girl	who
get	yes	give	woman

 /12 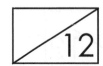 /12 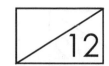 /12 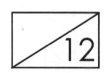 /12

Yes I can!

8

Sight Words

Basic Sight Vocabulary

Can I read these words?

List Five		**List Six**	
above	new	about	how
find	now	again	long
gave	over	always	or
got	put	any	them
has	round	ask	then
its	school	ate	they
know	so	cannot	walk
let	soon	could	went
live	ten	does	were
made	that	father	what
many	under	first	when
may	your	found	with

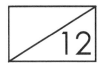 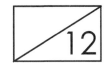 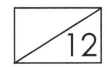 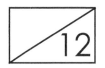

Yes I can!

Basic Sight Vocabulary

Can I read these words?

List Seven		**List Eight**	
because	once	brother	pull
been	open	buy	show
before	our	draw	sit
bring	say	drink	small
children	take	even	their
done	tell	fall	these
every	there	grow	think
goes	upon	hold	those
mother	us	hot	very
much	want	just	where
must	wish	keep	which
never	would	only	work

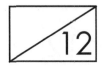 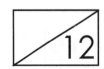 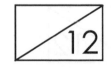 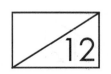

Yes I can!

Basic Sight Vocabulary

Can I read these words?

List Nine

best	pick
better	please
both	pretty
clean	read
cut	shall
eight	six
five	today
four	try
full	use
light	well
myself	why
off	write

List Ten

baby	sing
daughter	sister
far	sleep
house	something
hurt	son
kind	start
laugh	thank
Mr	together
Mrs	warm
own	wash
right	water
seven	white

 /12   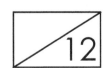 /12   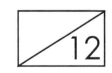 /12   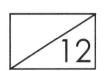 /12

Yes I can!

11

Learn these sounds

oo as in  oo as in

oi as in  oy as in

aw as in  au as in

ou as in ow as in

ow as in

(12)   and   are   boy

Unit 1:2

Circle the picture with the sound

can   come   funny   (13)

Unit 1:3

Circle the picture with the sound.

go   he   is

Write the missing letters.

br __ __ m	b __ __ l	st __ __ l
cr __ __ n	s __ __	h __ __ se

Underline the word for the picture.

1. moon   room   spoon   tool

2. wood   took   good   hook

3. show   row   bowl   own

4. cow   town   owl   growl

5. scoop   boot   shoot   room

jump   like   little   15

Write the missing letters.

t _ _ l	gr _ _ _	p _ _ _
c _ _ l	sh _ _ _	cr _ _ l
f _ _ l	m _ _ _	_ _ l
dr _ _ l	t _ _ _	fl _ _ _

Draw a line to match the words that rhyme.

food	brown	spoon	now
coin	scout	boil	soon
out	join	cow	drawn
town	mood	yawn	spoil

(16) look   my   of

Unit 1:6

Circle the word for the picture.

bowl bowls	spoon spoons
stool stools	cloud clouds

List the words with the same word pattern
under each picture.

spoil   grow   frown   foil   show

town   row   soil   crown

_____	_____	_____
_____	_____	_____
_____	_____	_____
_____	_____	_____
_____	_____	_____

play   red   run   17

Unit 1:7

Draw a line from the picture to the matching word.

mow	claw
slow	draw
bow	raw
out	row
spout	groom
shout	broom

Write the word that fits in the word shape box.

goose	noise	draw
troop	point	hawk
broom	spoil	crawl
stool	boil	yawn

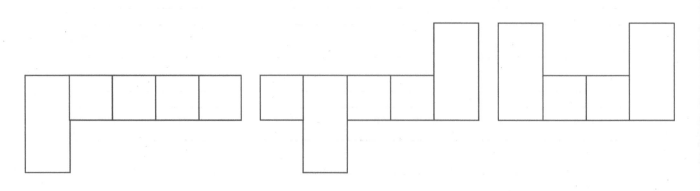

(18) said says see

Unit 1:8

Write the words for the pictures.

1 _____   2 _____   3 _____

4 _____   5 _____   6 _____

7 _____   8 _____   9 _____

the   this   to   ⑲

Unit 1:9

Tick the sentence that describes the picture.

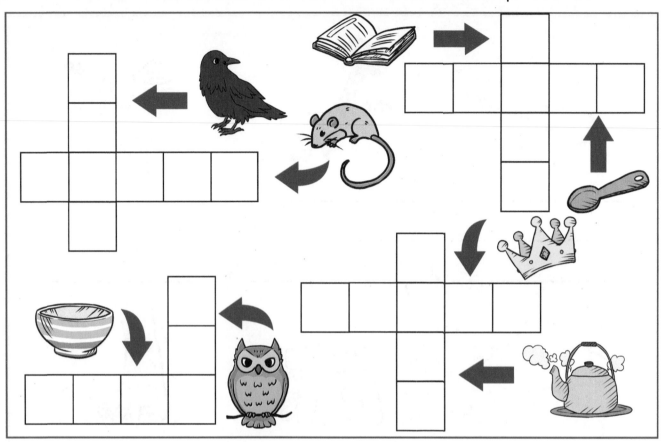

Write the words for the pictures.

1. Mum swept the steps with a . _____

2. The boys swam in the . _____

3. Paul fell off the of the house. _____

4. 'Hoot, Hoot.' said the . _____

5. We cut wood with a . _____

(20)   at   away   big

Unit 1:10

Diphthongs 10

Tick the sentence that describes the picture.

☐ A mouse in the snow.

☐ A mouse in the bowl.

☐ Stand in a pool.

☐ Stand on a stool.

☐ Tow the boat.

☐ Row the boat.

☐ Look at the moon.

☐ Look at the spoon.

☐ Throw the boot.

☐ Throw the hoop.

☐ A boy with toys.

☐ A boy with noise.

blue   down   for   ㉑

Write the words for the pictures.

1. _____	2. _____	3. _____
4. _____	5. _____	6. _____

Write the words from the box in the spaces.

roof	clowns	stool	spoons	foot

1. I stood on a _____ to get the food.

2. The book fell on my _____ .

3. An owl sat on the _____ of the house.

4. Mrs Law left the _____ in the sink.

5. The boys saw the _____ at the show.

(22) good   green   have   here

Unit 1:12

Diphthongs 12

Read the words as quickly and accurately as possible

Can I read these words?

cool	boom	moon	boot
pool	room	noon	hoot
tool	broom	soon	shoot
stool	groom	spoon	hoop
food	roof	goose	loop

good	book	oil	voice
hood	cook	boil	choice
wood	hook	spoil	noise
stood	look	coin	boy
foot	shook	join	toy

Time ⬜   ⬜/40 Right

Yes I can!

(23)

Unit 1:13

Read the words as quickly and accurately as possible

Can I read these words?

out	ounce	found	cow
shout	bounce	round	now
scout	count	sound	town
ouch	our	house	brown
couch	flour	mouse	owl

law	crawl	cause	low
paw	drawl	pause	row
raw	yawn	sauce	crow
saw	drawn	fault	slow
draw	hawk	haul	bowl

Time ☐     /40 Right

Yes I can!

Learn these sounds.

ar as in

er as in

ir as in

or as in

ur as in

in   it   man   me   25

Unit 2:2

Vowels before 'r' 2

Circle the picture with the sound.

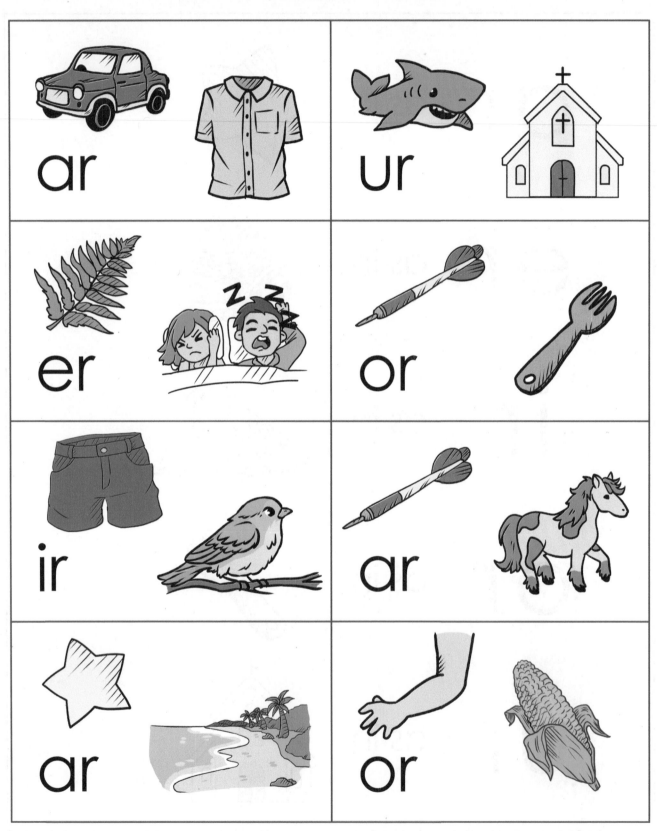

not   on   one   ran

Circle the picture with the sound.

ur	
ir	
or	
ar	
ar	
ir	
er	
or	

saw   three   too   up   27

Unit 2:4

Vowels before 'r' 4

Write the missing letters.

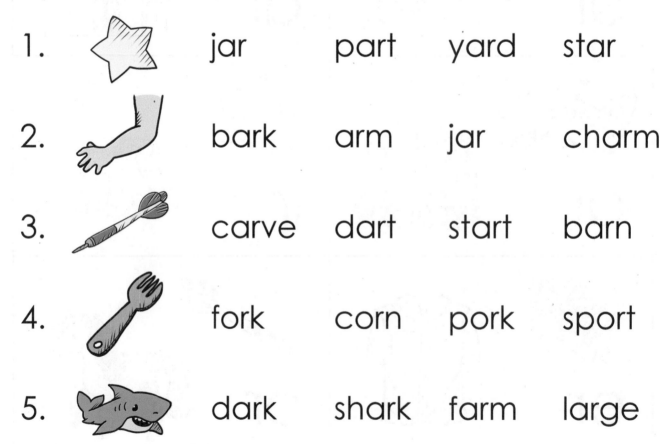

c _ _ _	b _ _ _ d	f _ _ _ k
f _ _ _ st	sh _ _ _ t	ch _ _ _ ch

Underline the word that matches the picture

1. jar   part   yard   star

2. bark   arm   jar   charm

3. carve   dart   start   barn

4. fork   corn   pork   sport

5. dark   shark   farm   large

(28)   watch   you   all   am

Unit 2:5

Vowels before 'r' 5

Write the missing letters.

b _ _ n	st _ _ _	sp _ _ k
th _ _ n	b _ _	d _ _ k
h _ _ n	f _ _	m _ _ k
t _ _ n	j _ _	b _ _ k

Draw a line to match the words that rhyme

card	shirt	more	turn
fern	third	porch	sore
bird	stern	fort	torch
skirt	yard	burn	sort

around   black   but   by   call   (29)

Unit 2:6

Vowels before 'r' 6

Circle the word for the picture.

horse horses	star stars
fork forks	fern ferns

List the words with the same word pattern under each picture.

born	start	bar	jar	torn
smart	far	horn	part	

came   do   eat   fast   get

Unit 2:7

Draw a line from the picture to the matching word.

skirt
squirt
shirt

store
shore
more

sports
sorts
shorts

snore
tore
chore

Write the word that fits in the word shape box.

score	nurse	girl
store	purse	firm
snore	churn	whirl
wore	turn	swirl

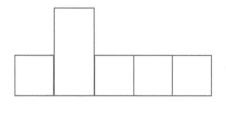
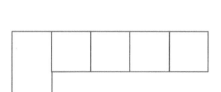

going   home   into   make   no   (31)

Unit 2:8

Write the words for the pictures.

1 _____

2 _____

3 _____

4 _____

5 _____

6 _____

7 _____

8 _____

9 _____

(32) old   out   was   we   will

Unit 2:9

Write the words for the pictures in the spaces shown by the arrows.

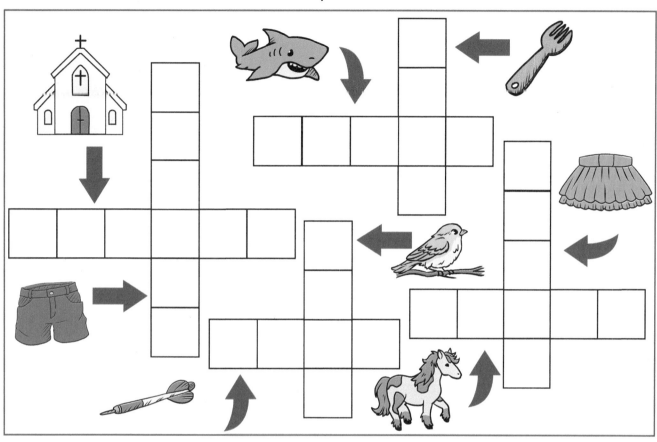

Write the words for the pictures.

1. The girl fell and hurt her . _____

2. Mark tore his best . _____

3. The shark swam past the  . _____

4. The dark 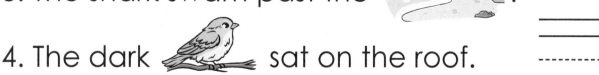 sat on the roof. _____

5. Bart ate his with a fork. _____

yellow   yes   an   after   as   (33)

Unit 2:10

Tick the sentence that describes the picture.

☐ A horse and dart.
☐ A horse and cart.

☐ A girl in shorts.
☐ A girl in sports.

☐ A bird on a perch.
☐ A bird in church

☐ My sore arm.
☐ My sore charm.

☐ Surf near the store.
☐ Surf near the shore.

☐ First piece of corn.
☐ Third piece of corn.

(34) be   brown   cold   did   ever

Unit 2:11

Write the words for the pictures.

1. _____
2. _____
3. _____
4. _____
5. _____
6. _____

Write the words from the box in the space.

skirt   born   yard   girl   car

1. The _____ was hard to start.

2. Our dog barks in the back _____ .

3. Mum tore her _____ on the thorn.

4. I was _____ on the third of March.

5. The first _____ ran down to the park.

| fly | from | girl | give | had | (35) |

Unit 2:12

Vowels before 'r' 12

Read the words as quickly and accurately as possible

Can I read these words?

car	dark	arm	dart	jerk
far	park	farm	part	her
star	shark	charm	start	perch
hard	large	barn	carve	germ
yard	charge	snarl	starve	fern

sir	girl	more	fork	spur
stir	firm	sore	porch	church
bird	shirt	shore	born	surf
third	skirt	store	corn	hurt
first	birth	horse	short	burn

Time ☐   ☐ / 50 Right

Yes I can!

36

Learn these sounds.

air   as in      are   as in   

ear   as in      ea   as in

our   as in   oar   as in   

all   as in      al   as in   

or   as in      ear   as in   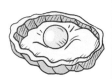

ew   as in   ue   as in   

oor   as in      ear   as in   

help   her   him   his   if   (37)

Circle the picture with the long vowel sound.

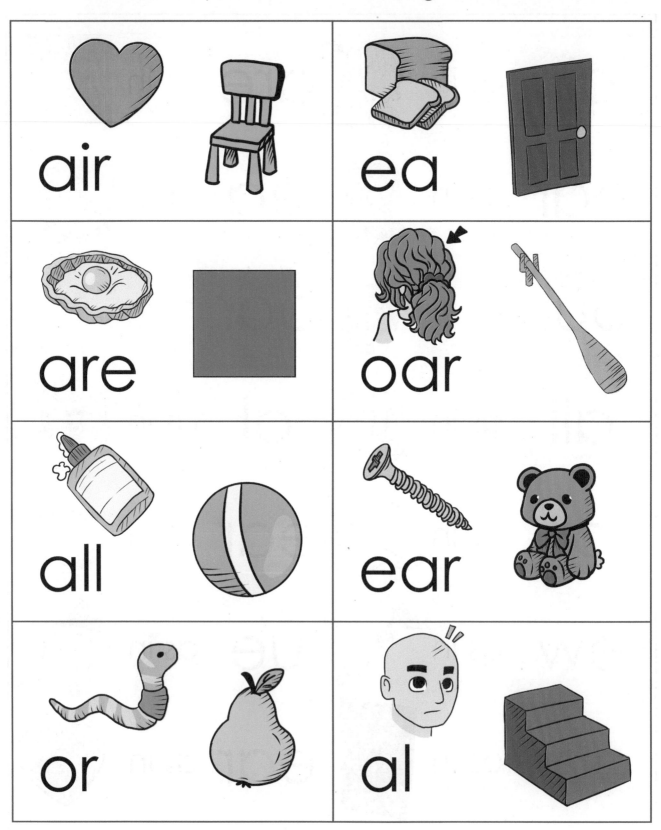

air | ea

are | oar

all | ear

or | al

she   some   stop   two   who

Unit 3:3

Circle the picture with the long vowel sound.

woman   above   find   gave   got   39

Write the missing letters.

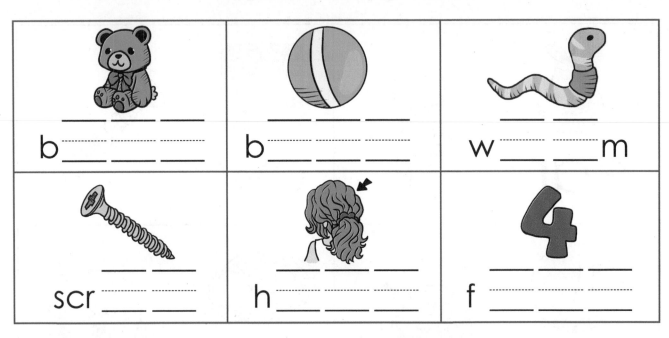

b _____   b _____   w __ __m

scr __ __ __   h _____   f _____

Underline the word that matches the picture

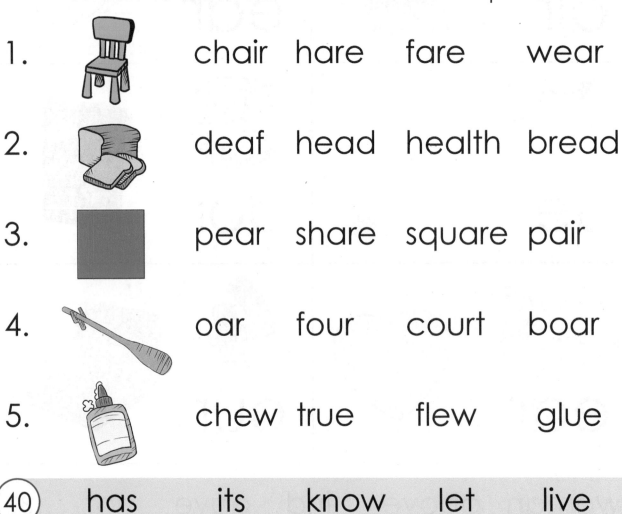

1. chair   hare   fare   wear

2. deaf   head   health   bread

3. pear   share   square   pair

4. oar   four   court   boar

5. chew   true   flew   glue

(40) has   its   know   let   live

Write the missing letters.

b _____	f _____	p _____
f _____	st _____	w _____
t _____	p _____	t _____
sm _____	h _____	sw _____

Draw a line to match the words that rhyme

oar	share	cue	pour
care	flew	sweat	due
head	bread	salt	threat
blew	roar	four	malt

made   many   may   new   now (41)

Unit 3:6

Circle the word for the picture.

door doors	pear pears
pearl pearls	heart hearts

List the words with the same word pattern
under each picture.

fall   head   read   rare   wall

thread   care   spare   small

over   put   round   school   so

Draw a line from the picture to the matching word.

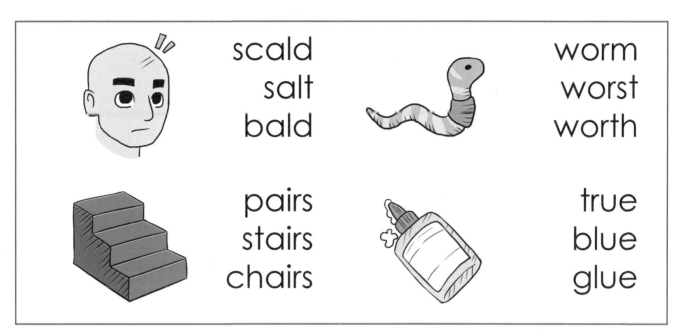

scald
salt
bald

worm
worst
worth

pairs
stairs
chairs

true
blue
glue

Write the word that fits in the word shape box.

course

court

fourth

pour

work

worm

world

worst

pearl

learn

earth

heard

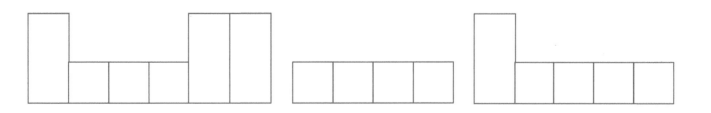

soon   ten   that   under   your   (43)

Write the words for the pictures.

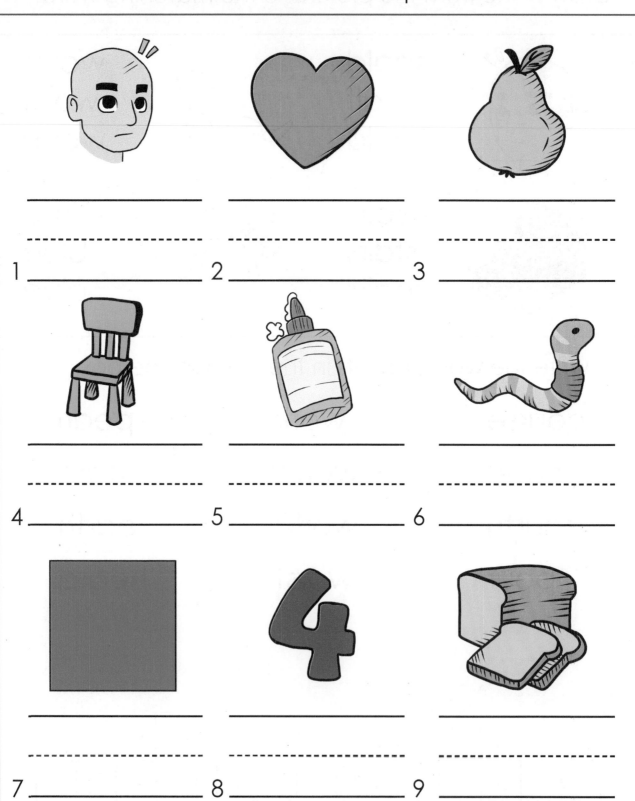

1 _____

2 _____

3 _____

4 _____

5 _____

6 _____

7 _____

8 _____

9 _____

about again always any ask

Write the words for the pictures in the spaces
shown by the arrows.

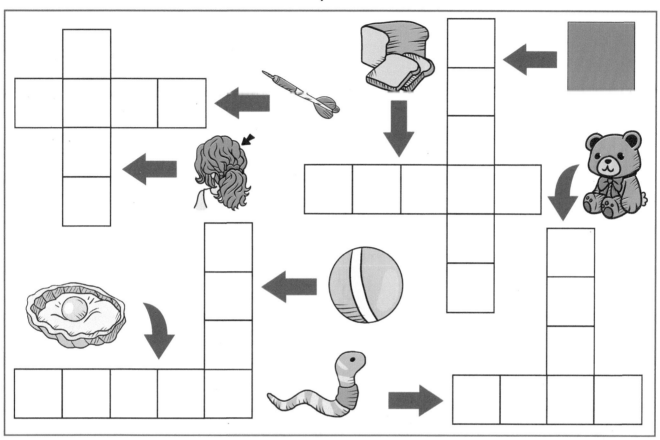

Write the words for the pictures.

1. The blue was by the stairs. _____

2. Mum threw out the stale . _____

3. The man had a cold head. _____

4. Clare hit the 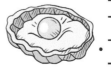 out of the court. _____

5. The girl will search for the lost ⬤. _____

ate   cannot   could   does   father   (45)

Unit 3:10

Digraphs 10

Tick the sentence that describes the picture.

☐ Bread on a thread

☐ Bread on my head.

☐ Share a chair.

☐ Wear a chair.

☐ Eat four pears.

☐ Eat four bears.

☐ The fourth door.

☐ The fourth floor.

☐ A worm in my hair

☐ A worrn In the air.

☐ A girl with glue.

☐ A girl with pearls.

46 first   found   how   long   or

Write the words for the pictures.

1. ----------------	2. ----------------	3. ----------------
4. ----------------	5. ----------------	6. ----------------

Write the words from the box in the space.

threw	roar	heard	stairs	world

1. Clark heard the wild bear _____.

2. Take care when you run down _____ .

3. The boys _____ the ball at the door.

4. The jet plane flew round the _____ .

5. I _____ the worst news.

them	then	they	walk	went	(47)

Read the words as quickly and accurately as possible

Can I read these words?

oar	earn	word	care	bear
roar	learn	work	dare	pear
court	heard	worm	rare	fair
four	pearl	world	scare	hair
door	search	worst	share	chair

ball	head	sweat	flew	new
call	read	meant	drew	few
small	bread	breath	screw	stew
bald	spread	health	blue	cue
salt	thread	wealth	true	due

Time [ ]  /50 Right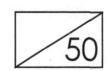

Yes I can!

Learn these silent letters.

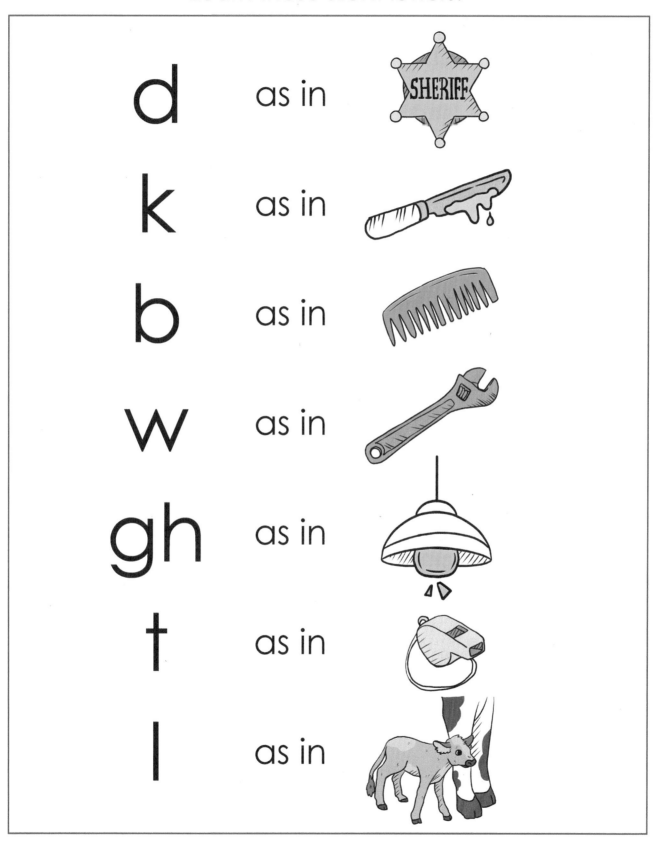

d   as in   SHERIFF

k   as in

b   as in

w   as in

gh   as in

t   as in

l   as in

Unit 4:2

Circle the letters you do **not** hear.

n b k	u b m
w t r	gh l i
l t c	m p l
b o m	n k e

(50) been   before   bring   children   done

Circle the letters you do **not** hear.

d b a	n i k
r w ch	w l k
i wh t	l f c
r d i	s or w

every   goes   mother   much   must   51

Unit 4:4

Write the missing letters.

wa __ k   s __ ord   cas __ le

li __ __ t   ca __ f   we __ ge

Underline the word that matches the picture

1.    sign   bright   weigh   knight

2.    crumb   lamb   thumb   climb

3.    wrestle   bristle   whistle   hustle

4.   walk   palm   yolk   balm

5.   eight   night   bought   freight

never   once   open   our   say

Unit 4:5

Write the missing letters.

bri___t	___nit	bri___ge
ti___t	___nee	ju___ge
ni___t	___neel	e___ge
si___t	___new	do___ge

Draw a line to match the words that rhyme

judge	glisten	right	freight
numb	talk	bought	light
listen	thumb	eight	calf
walk	fudge	half	thought

take   tell   there   upon   us   (53)

Unit 4:6

Circle the word for the picture.

knob knobs

comb combs

badge badges

bomb bombs

List the words with the same word pattern under each picture.

talk	tight	hedge	chalk	ledge
right	edge	stalk	night	

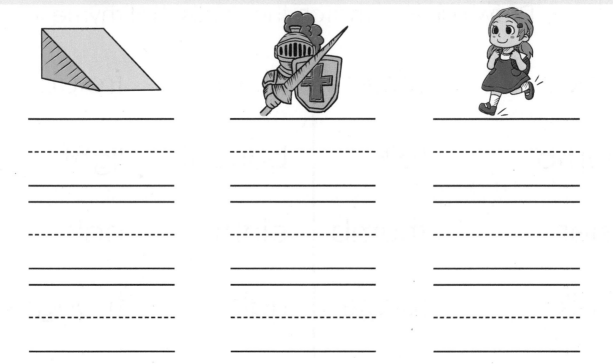

want wish would brother buy

Unit 4:7

Draw a line from the picture to the matching word.

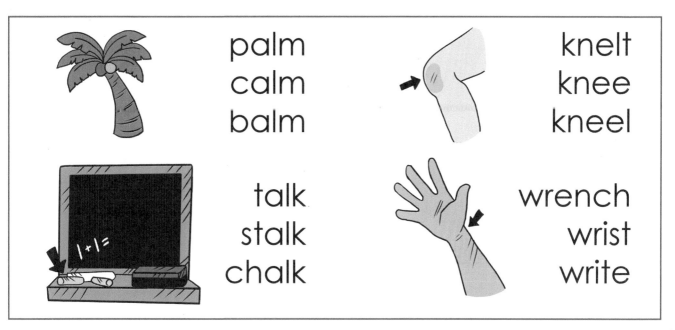

palm
calm
balm

knelt
knee
kneel

talk
stalk
chalk

wrench
wrist
write

Write the word that fits in the word shape box.

castle	weigh	lamb
whistle	weight	numb
bristle	sleigh	thumb
nestle	freight	crumb

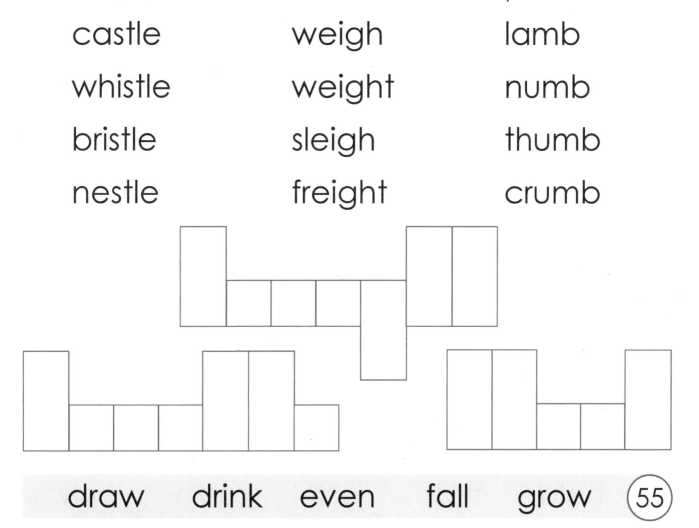

draw   drink   even   fall   grow   (55)

Unit 4:8

Write the words for the pictures.

1 _____

2 _____

3 _____

4 _____

5 _____

6 _____

7 _____

8 _____

9 _____

hold   hot   just   keep   only

Unit 4:9

Write the words for the pictures in the spaces
shown by the arrows.

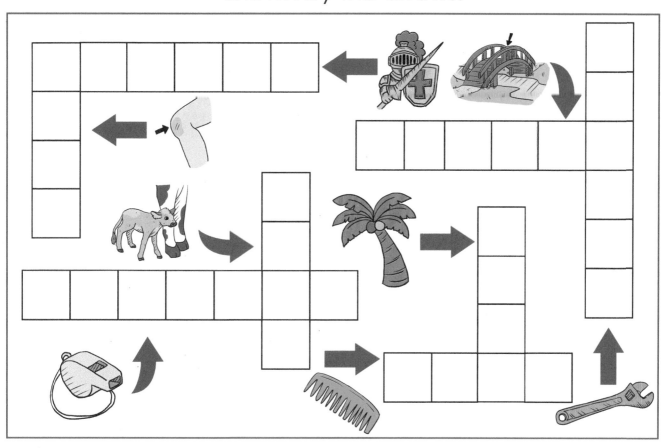

Write the words for the pictures.

1. The knights rode out of the ⬛ .

2. Can I write with a piece of ⬛ ?

3. We caught fish.

4. I will try to climb the 🌴 tree.

5. Tim thought he heard a .

pull   show   sit   small   their   57

Unit 4:10

Tick the sentence that describes the picture.

☐ A bright flight.
☐ A bright light.

☐ A knock on the door
☐ A knob on the door.

☐ Eight kids in a sleigh.
☐ Eight kids in the weight

☐ Walk and chalk.
☐ Walk and talk

☐ Climb the palm tree.
☐ Climb the half tree.

☐ Sleep sight at night.
☐ Sleep tight at night.

(58) these   think   those   very   where

Unit 4:11

Write the words for the pictures.

1. _____	2. _____	3. _____
4. _____	5. _____	6. _____

Write the words from the box in the space.

knock   right   taught   know   walk

1. Mr Wright _____ the class to read.

2. I thought I should go for a _____ .

3. 'Listen, I hear a _____ on the door.'

4. He held a sword in his _____ hand.

5. Do you _____ how to spell eight words?

which   work   best   better   both   (59)

Unit 4:12

Silent letters 12

Read the words as quickly and accurately as possible

Can I read these words?

edge	knit	lamb	wrench	light
ledge	knob	bomb	wrist	night
badge	knee	thumb	wrong	knight
bridge	knife	comb	write	bright
judge	know	climb	sword	high

sleigh	bought	castle	balk	balm
weigh	brought	nestle	talk	calm
eight	thought	whistle	walk	palm
weight	caught	bristle	chalk	calf
freight	taught	hustle	stalk	half

Time [   ]    /50 Right

Yes I can!

More work with words

Unit 5:2

Write the missing letters.

b __ __ k   cl __ __ n   sn __ __ e

b __ __ r   com __   b __ __

Underline the word that matches the picture

1.   rare   hair   bear   pair

2.   boil   spoil   boy   toy

3.   farm   dark   shark   barn

4.   chalk   calm   calf   walk

5.   cool   took   pool   shook

(62)   full   light   myself   off   pick

Write the missing letters.

thr ___ ___ ___	s ___ ___ n	sh ___ ___ ___
bl ___ ___ ___	n ___ ___ n	sp ___ ___ ___
dr ___ ___ ___	m ___ ___ n	gl ___ ___ ___
fl ___ ___ ___	cr ___ ___ n	r ___ ___ ___

Draw a line to match the words that rhyme

blue	thirst	claw	boy
blow	charm	toy	shore
first	throw	bought	draw
farm	true	store	thought

please   pretty   read   shall   six   (63)

Unit 5:4

Circle the word for the picture.

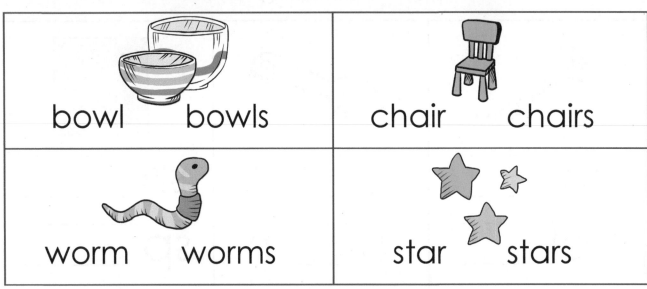

bowl bowls	chair chairs
worm worms	star stars

List the words with the same word pattern
under each picture.

frown   head   hall   read   town

fall   brown   tall   thread

_____	_____	_____

today   try   use   well   why

Unit 5:5

Draw a line from the picture to the matching word.

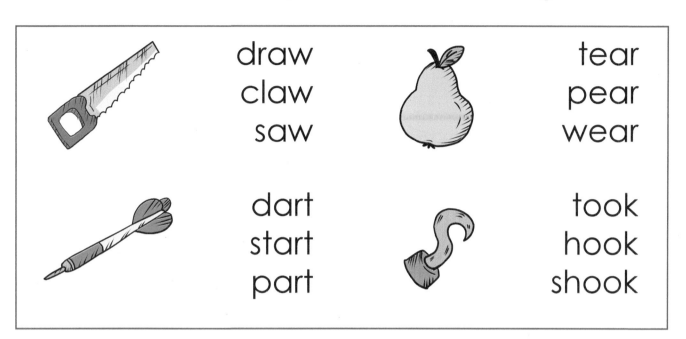

draw
claw
saw

tear
pear
wear

dart
start
part

took
hook
shook

Write the word that fits in the word shape box.

badge   work   bound

bridge   worth   pound

grudge   worst   sound

pledge   world   ground

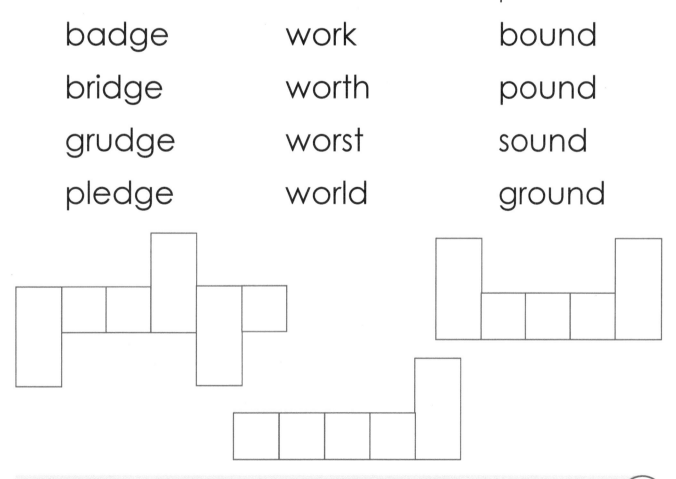

write   baby   daugther   for   house   65

Unit 5:6

Write the words for the pictures.

1 _____   2 _____   3 _____

4 _____   5 _____   6 _____

7 _____   8 _____   9 _____

hurt   kind   laugh   Mr   Mrs

Five Senses Phonics Book 6

Unit 5:7

Revision Unit

Write the words for the pictures in the spaces
shown by the arrows.

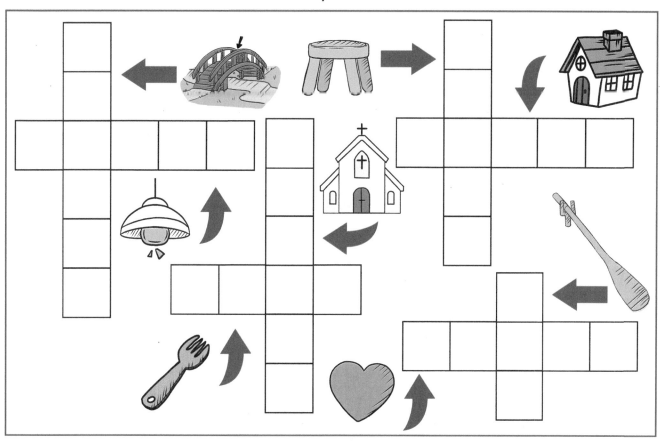

Write the words for the pictures.

1. The cook cut the with a knife. _____

2. Clare fell off her . _____

3. I wrote eight words in my  . _____

4. Dad cut the boards with a . _____

5. Can an  hoot In the woods? _____

own   right   seven   sing   sister

Tick the sentence that describes the picture.

☐ Look at the cook.
☐ Look at my book.

☐ Comb my hair.
☐ Comb the stairs.

☐ A sore knee.
☐ A sore knot.

☐ A fork and moon.
☐ A fork and spoon.

☐ A snooze in a chair.
☐ A snooze on the stairs.

☐ Bread in the south.
☐ Bread in my mouth.

sleep   something   son   start   thank

Write the words for the pictures.

1. _____	2. _____	3. _____
4. _____	5. _____	6. _____

Write the words from the box in the space.

caught   nurse   house   knee   loose

1. The knot was too _____ to hold the calf.

2. Paul hurt his _____ when he ran.

3. Mr Dark will weigh the fish he _____ .

4. The _____ took care of Mum's sore wrist.

5. Last March we bought a new _____ .

together   warm   wash   water   white   (69)

Read the words as quickly and accurately as possible

 Can I read these words?

pool	good	coin	shout	cow
broom	wood	join	couch	now
spoon	foot	point	bounce	owl
shoot	book	voice	found	town
loop	shook	boy	mouse	brown

raw	row	car	her	fir
draw	blow	yard	jerk	bird
crawl	snow	bark	germ	girl
yawn	flown	farm	fern	skirt
fault	bowl	start	nerve	birth

Time    50   Right

Yes I can!

(70)

Unit 5:11

Read the words as quickly and accurately as possible

Can I read these words?

horse	spur	roar	care	ball
more	surf	four	square	small
cork	church	door	hair	salt
corn	burn	pearl	chair	bald
sport	nurse	worm	bear	bread

flew	ledge	comb	light	listen
chew	badge	thumb	bright	soften
new	bridge	climb	eight	castle
true	knot	wrong	bought	talk
blue	knee	write	taught	palm

Time     /50   Right

Yes I can!

(71)

Achievement Tests

The Five Senses Phonics Achievement Tests complement each book in the Five Senses Phonics series. They are specifically designed to enable teachers to ensure that what has been taught remains current in the student's repertoire of skills. They can then identify areas that need reteaching or reinforcement.

The format of each Five Senses Phonics Achievement Test is identical to the equivalent book so students encounter activities with which they are familiar. Each test evaluates skills and sight words students have been taught. The careful design of the tests, ensures that the monitoring of progress is a positive and non-threatening exercise.

For ease of administration, the tests are photocopiable. The class record sheets and student record sheets allow the teacher to scan student performance on an individual or whole class basis. Taken as a group, the tests give a running record of each student's skill acquisition of the phonic hierarchy. Teachers who teach reading systematically and record student progress methodically will find the Five Senses Phonics First Achievement Tests an indispensable part of their teaching routine.

How to use these tests

The Five Senses Phonics Achievement Tests are intended to be an encouraging record of progress, not an intimidating assessment. The tests can be administered to individual students or the entire class. Allow approximately 30 minutes to complete each test.

Each group of tests contains one or two sight vocabulary tests. If administering the test to the class as a whole, have individual students read groups of sight words, then ask the class to read all sight words together. Keep watch for children who are having trouble, and test them later individually.

Maintain a positive attitude while administering the tests, and reward success with stickers, stamps and merit certificates. To attain mastery students should obtain at least 80 marks out of a possible 100. Any areas in the Test that indicate weakness should be retaught and then reinforced.

Test Record Sheet

Student .... Date...

Page	Test		
74	1	Word completion; word recognition	/11
75	2	Singular-plural; recognising word patterns	/13
76	3	Word recognition; word shape boxes	/7
77	4	Spelling	/9
78	5	Crossword puzzles; word completion	/9
79	6	Sentence comprehension	/6
80	7	Singular-plural spelling; sentence completion	/11
81	8	Reading digraphs, Diphthongs, Vowels before ~r', Silent letter words	/34

Knowledge of digraphs, Diphthongs, Vowels before 'r', Silent letter words **Total** /100

| 82 | 9 | **Basic Sight vocabulary** | /40 |

Test 6:1

Word completion; word recognition

Write the missing letters.

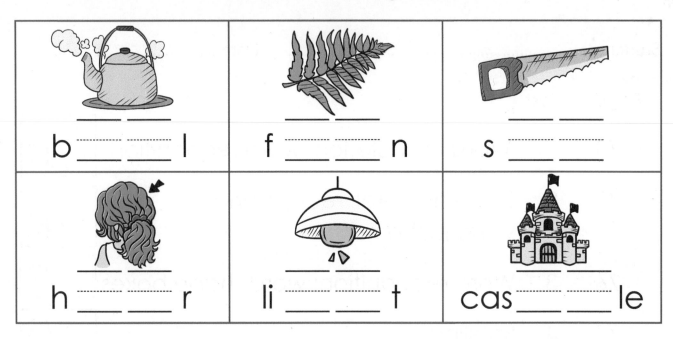

b _____ l	f _____ n	s _____
h _____ r	li _____ t	cas _____ le

Underline the word that matches the picture

1. cow   owl   crown   town

2. dart   charm   start   farm

3. hoot   shoot   room   boot

4. door   four   pour   floor

5. lamb   crumb   thumb   limb

(74)

Score   / 11

Test 6:2

Singular-plural; recognising word patterns

Circle the word for the picture.

bird birds	bowl bowls
pear pears	knob knobs

List the words with the same word pattern under each picture.

grow   born   low   call   thorn

small   row   torn   fall

Score   ☐ / 13

Test 6:3

Word recognition; word shape boxes

Draw a line from the picture to the matching word.

rare
square
share

snore
store
more

blue
true
glue

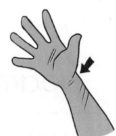

wrong
wrist
write

Write the word that fits in the word shape box.

purse	worm	chalk
turn	work	walk
curl	worst	calf
nurse	world	talk

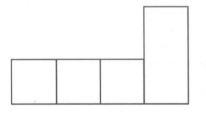

(76)

Score ☐ / 9

Test 6:4

Spelling

Write the words for the pictures.

1 _____

2 _____

3 _____

4 _____

5 _____

6 _____

7 _____

8 _____

9 _____

Score / 9

Test 6:5

Crossword puzzles; word completion

Write the words for the pictures in the spaces shown by the arrows.

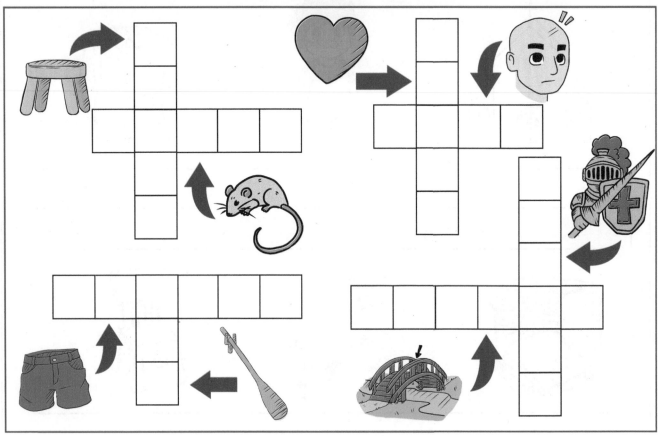

Write the words for the pictures.

1. Paul has a new in his room. ....

2. Mrs Knight wore her ring. ....

3. Mark saw a  in the surf. ....

4. The girl fell and tore her  . ...

5. Claire left her in the car. ....

Score ☐ /9

Test 6:6

Sentence comprehension

Tick the sentence that describes the picture.

☐ My sore farm hurts.

☐ My sore arm hurts.

☐ The boy has lots of toys.

☐ The boy has no toys.

☐ The girl wears her pearls.

☐ The girl tears her pearls.

☐ The light is not tight.

☐ The light is too bright.

☐ I can eat four pears.

☐ I can eat four chairs.

☐ She knocks on the door.

☐ She knocks on the floor.

Score ☐ / 6

Test 6:7

Singular-plural spelling; sentence completion

Write the words for the pictures.

1. _____

2. _____

3. _____

4. _____

5. _____

6. _____

Write the words from the box in the space.

| stairs | words | books | sword | shirt |

1. Carl tore his _____ on the sharp thorn.

2. The boys ran down the back _____.

3. Four _____ fell on my head.

4. I know how to spell lots of _____.

5. Can a knight fight with a _____?

Score ⬚ /11

Test 6:8

Reading consonant and vowel digraphs.

Oral reading test

Read the words as quickly and accurately as possible.

pool	park	fern	knit
claw	book	share	torch
third	house	boil	hurt
hair	bald	blue	toy
comb	shout		

grow	bridge	worm	roar
bear	brown	clown	moon
fall	bread	church	snore
eight	foot	four	pearl

Score / 34

(81)

Test 6:9

Basic Sight Vocabulary

Read the words as quickly and accurately as possible.

better	four	off	use
both	full	pretty	why
eight	light	today	write
clean	myself	read	why
best	five	please	try
daughter	right	sleep	together
house	son	start	wash
something	seven	far	white
baby	laugh	sister	water
hurt	sing	thank	warm

Time [   ]   [/ 40] Right

Score [/ 40]